99
THOUGHTS
ON MARRIAGE
& MINISTRY

PRIORITIZING THE
"HOLY MESS" OF
MATRIMONY

JAKE & MELISSA KIRCHER

YouthMinistry.com/TOGETHER

99 Thoughts on Marriage & Ministry
Prioritizing the "HolyMess" of Matrimony

© 2013 Jake and Melissa Kircher

group.com
simplyyouthministry.com

Credits
Authors: Jake and Melissa Kircher
Executive Developer: Nadim Najm
Chief Creative Officer: Joani Schultz
Editor: Rob Cunningham
Cover Art and Production: Veronica Preston
Author Photo: Alex Christine Photography (alex-christine.com)

ISBN 978-0-7644-9135-1

10 9 8 7 6 5 4 3 2 1   20 19 18 17 16 15 14 13

Printed in the United States of America.

Dedicated to Glenn...

TABLE OF CONTENTS

INTRODUCTION: MARRIAGE AND MINISTRY

Couples who hold church leadership or staff positions often believe that they shouldn't have any problems, especially when it comes to marriage and family. If someone were to find out how imperfect they really were, it would mean that they'd be considered unfit for their job or role. However, this mindset is completely false.

We've had numerous conversations with ministry couples who really struggle in their marriages and feel embarrassed and alone in their problems. Ministry has a propensity to demand much from us professionally, personally, and spiritually. Trust us, if you're struggling, you are not alone!

We like to define marriage as a "holymess." The holy parts of a relationship go hand in hand with the messy parts—and, in fact, you can't have one without the other. The times when things are great get us through the rough patches, and the rough patches help us learn, grow, and pull closer together.

This book stems from our own personal holymess. We share these thoughts with you because we've learned them all the hard way! Some days it feels like all we do is fail. Yet every mess, problem, heartache, and struggle has matured us individually and as a couple. And we'll keep on learning. It's a process, this marriage thing.

We hope and pray that *99 Thoughts on Ministry & Marriage* will challenge both you and your spouse, and encourage you to work toward a strong, healthy, holymess marriage.

Jake and Melissa

SECTION 1

MARRIAGE BASICS

One of the biggest lessons we've learned so far is that ministry should never come before marriage.

Five years ago, Jake was a part-time youth pastor working more than 70 hours a week between his church position and two side jobs. He burned out fast. This took a huge toll on our marriage. It was very difficult to accept that after only two years of marriage, our relationship was crumbling. We recognized that we needed help. As we got professional counseling and began to share the truth about our relationship with friends, we realized that our priorities and pace of life were not honoring to God. We had ignored our marriage for the sake of the church and it only brought destruction.

As we transitioned to a new church, we began to put our marriage first. The amazing thing was that both our marriage and the ministry were the better for it! Here are a number of the things we've learned from counselors, friends, books, and seminars about the basics of keeping a marriage healthy and putting it first.

4 THOUGHTS ON KEEPING ROMANCE ALIVE

1. DON'T WAIT UNTIL IT'S TOO LATE

If it isn't broken, don't fix it. Many people use this motto when they think about marriage, but couples who ignore their relationship until problems surface do so at their own peril. A good marriage is a proactive one. This means that romance, intimacy, and connection should be a daily consideration of both spouses. Couples should make regular, consistent efforts to foster these three key ingredients of a healthy marriage. For example, both spouses can work on saying affirming things to each other every day, can talk over the dinner table, or can engage in a long, passionate kiss before leaving for work. The danger in letting your marriage slide is that problems often start out small but fester and grow until the gap between you and your spouse has widened to serious proportions. Don't wait until it's too late; do something today to encourage romance, intimacy, and connection in your marriage.

2. TRY NEW THINGS

Part of the fun in marriage (and life) is trying new things together. This could be as simple as sampling food from another country for the first time or as involved as planning a trip to another country. Couples might want to be even more adventurous and try things that confront their fears, such as jumping out of a plane or going whitewater rafting. Whatever it is, make sure to do it as a team. When a couple can share new experiences, overcome challenges, and create unique memories together, the relationship becomes fun and exciting. Intimacy is forged during these times, and the fires of passion are often stirred up. Never underestimate the power of trying something new.

3. KEEP DATE NIGHT FRESH

The healthy habit of weekly date nights is familiar to many couples. But even when these dates are scheduled and prioritized, they can begin to feel stale and routine. It is hard to figure out what to do week after week. Here are a few creative date night ideas to keep things fresh:

- Get dressed up and go out for dinner at a fast food joint, and then go to a local arcade for some air hockey and video games—extra points if you wear heels and a suit.

- Use a GPS or phone to pick a random restaurant and go there. Make sure you're both in a flexible mood, as part of the fun is getting lost and trying new things.

- Search online or dig through a cookbook for new recipes. Head to the grocery store to get the ingredients and then cook the meal together. Enjoy with a glass of your favorite beverage and a movie.

Want more? Visit holymessofmarriage.com and click on "Creative Date Night Ideas," where you can find an idea for every week of the year.

4. DUAL RESPONSIBILITY

In many marriages, one spouse expects the other to initiate romance. But not only is this expectation unfair, it also can create serious tension. Both spouses need to initiate romance, which includes communication, flirting, thoughtfulness, quality time, and sex. It's the job of both the husband and wife to make their significant other feel loved and wanted, and to make the effort to keep intimacy alive in the relationship. No doubt about it, romance takes effort, especially after a couple has been married for a while. If the effort isn't shared, one spouse will feel exhausted and resentful, and the other will feel hurt and angry. Couples shouldn't worry about what the other spouse is or isn't doing but should take ownership of their own actions and initiate romance without expecting anything in return. If both can do this, the relationship will become balanced, healthy, and full of tenderness and love.

5 WAYS TO CONNECT WITH EACH OTHER

6. THE FIVE LOVE LANGUAGES

In his book *The Five Love Languages*, Gary Chapman explains the main methods that people use to give or receive love:

1. Physical touch (which includes more than just sex)

2. Gifts

3. Acts of service

4. Words of affirmation

5. Quality time

It is important to identify your own love language and also to understand the love language of your spouse. Typically, a person has one main way they feel loved and then shows love to others using the same method. If Melissa needs quality time to feel loved, she also shows love to Jake by giving him quality time—even though his love language is words of affirmation. Spouses can feel disconnected and unloved simply because they are speaking their own love language, instead of the other person's language. Learn to speak your spouse's language, too.

6. BUSINESS MEETING

Marriage can often feel like a business. On a daily basis, couples must hash out schedules, finances, job issues, home needs, kids, errands, and so on. It becomes easy to allow these things to take over life and dominate conversations. When this happens, it's natural to feel emotionally disconnected from each other. A healthy way to handle this problem is to have a regular business meeting once a week, every other week, or once a month—whatever works best for your needs. During this meeting, tackle as many of the decisions and business-type issues as you can. Obviously, immediate needs will pop up during the week and have to be addressed, but having a regular business meeting will cut down on the amount of time you spend each day discussing responsibilities and will free up that time for fun conversations. We have found it very helpful to have our business meetings during walks. Being outside and active keeps tensions low and the conversation focused on the issues at hand.

7. KEEP IT LIGHT

Another way to avoid a stale marriage is to have fun together. Laugh together when your kids say something ridiculous, go out for ice cream, flirt as you make dinner, try a new dog park, make a mess, buy something frivolous, go hiking, or find a hidden beach. Do whatever you and your spouse need to do to have fun. Keep it light, and you'll be all right for the long haul.

8. MAKE OUT

A friend of ours likes to joke, "Dating couples—you think you can't keep your hands off each other? Well, guess what? You can! Just get married!" There is something about the human condition that finds forbidden things exciting. When sex becomes permissible, some of the intoxicating feelings surrounding it wear off. As a way to reconnect and remind each other about the exciting times when blood was hot and it felt impossible not to touch each other, make time to make out. Seriously, put this book down right now and *go make out* with your spouse! Kissing without it leading to sex is a great way for couples to rediscover racing hearts, sweaty palms, and the wonderful feeling of wanting more.

9. MARS AND VENUS

Author John Gray wrote the bestselling book *Men Are From Mars, Women Are From Venus* to describe how men and women think and communicate differently. While it is true that there are some core gender differences, these broader classifications can be frustrating to implement in real life. It's better to focus on the fact that husbands and wives usually have unique methods of communication that confuse and frustrate one another—methods that often have nothing to do with gender.

Husbands and wives need to be aware of their individual communication styles. They should make an effort to help their spouse understand their unique way of talking and interacting and give suggestions as to what types of responses would be most beneficial.

It's also helpful to understand how each spouse processes information. A person who processes things verbally will most likely repeat the same ideas over and over and will want feedback to help reach a conclusion. A person who processes internally will often communicate in short, direct sentences and not want any feedback.

The key is to be self-aware, patient, and kind. The internal processor will have to learn to quell their impatience at the seemingly endless circular chatter of their mate, and the external processor will have to learn to not interrupt their spouse when they share their carefully considered thoughts. Give and take. Love and respect. These are the tools to good communication that often takes a lifetime to learn but is so worth the effort.

4 WAYS TO HAVE A HEALTHY SEX LIFE

We've never met a couple who hasn't struggled with their sex life in one way or another. Healthy sex requires intimacy, romance, and connection. If things in the bedroom are not too hot, it is possibly because one or more of these things are missing. Instead of trying to come up with specific solutions about sex, you may need to take a step back, re-read Thoughts 1-9, and do some basic relationship maintenance in your marriage.

Beyond those three key ingredients, here are four other thoughts to help your marriage in the bedroom.

10. EXPLAIN EXPECTATIONS

When we first got married, we expected sex to be this awesome, fulfilling, romantic, and passionate thing that we would do ALL THE TIME—at least for the first year or so. It took exactly one night together for us to realize that reality doesn't live up to fantasy. Sex takes work, just like every other part of the marriage relationship. The first step in working toward a healthy sex life is to understand each other's expectations.

Here are some helpful questions to talk about together:

- How often do you each want sex?

- How much and what kind of foreplay do you want?

- How do you want your spouse to initiate sex?

- What kind of sex do you want? (speed, positions, and so on)

- What does being satisfied sexually mean?

- What do you want to have happen after sex?

The goal is to understand what each spouse desires and then to work together to lovingly meet each other's needs and find ways to compromise. This expectation conversation is one you will have many times throughout the life of your marriage. Generally, it's helpful to check in and talk about sex at least once a month.

11. SCHEDULE IT

Schedule sex? But doesn't that take all the fun and romance out of it? Yes, sometimes. But we've learned that when life gets hectic, scheduled sex is better than no sex at all! Also, having a set date and time on the calendar can reduce initiation pressure and create an environment where both spouses are prepared and excited. Pick days that are usually open and free of responsibilities, or times when the house is quiet and the kids are in bed.

We also found it helpful to come up with a code word to refer to sex. This allowed us to talk, text, email, or use social media to communicate about our plans without fear of a student seeing a text or a co-worker catching part of our conversation. For a season in our life, some people just assumed that playing Scrabble® was a regular part of our marriage!

12. SPICE IT UP

After years of marriage, sex can become a little bit predictable and mundane. Create times when you make the effort to spice things up. God is our creator and has made his children creative people. It is our humble opinion that bedroom activities should include only you and your spouse and shouldn't cause physical or emotional harm. After that, go ahead and be a little wild. Try new positions and locations; just make sure you're in agreement about what's OK and what's not.

If you're looking for ideas and resources, we recommend checking out the Christian website covenantspice.com.

13. GUARANTEED SATISFACTION

Many couples are scared to talk about sexual satisfaction; there is a great fear of failure surrounding this issue. Sex is often tied to the male ego and a female's perceived desirability, and none of us wants to think about falling short. However, most issues in the bedroom don't stem from a lack of manliness or beauty; they stem from emotional problems, fatigue, worry, stress, or miscommunication about expectations or desires. Sex is the physical expression of the emotional connection in a relationship, and many things can affect this connection both positively and negatively.

When talking about sexual satisfaction, remember to approach any issues gently. Be compassionate and understanding with each other. Try to get to the root of any problems as well. Is a lack of desire coming from longer hours at work or because one spouse has stopped exercising? Does one spouse want to try new things in the bedroom but is hesitant to share their desires? Your marriage should be a safe place to talk about sexual satisfaction, and both spouses need to focus on loving solutions and compromises rather than accusations.

3 MUSTS TO MAINTAIN SEXUAL PURITY

14. POWER IN NUMBERS

One of the best ways to maintain sexual purity in life and marriage is for both spouses to find accountability partners. They should connect regularly with these partners over coffee, on the phone, via email, or even by text. Having a trusted friend who will check in and ask about purity is a great way to help avoid temptations and foster holy minds, hearts, and lifestyles.

16. CHECKS AND BALANCES

People today are surrounded by technology and there is a huge increase in the number of opportunities for easily accessing pornography and/or sexually explicit material. Because of this, it is crucial to set up checks and balances for your marriage and family. Here are a handful of ideas to consider:

- Make sure every computer has Internet filters and accountability software installed. Safe Eyes and X3Watch are two great programs we would recommend.

- Put desktop computers in high-traffic areas of the home.

- Disable the Wi-Fi signal (check your router manual) or turn off any Internet gadgets after a certain time of night.

- Get rid of premium cable channels.

- Make sure every handheld device that connects to the Internet has an accountability app. X3Watch from XXXchurch.com is a great resource.

- Decide if setting up password-protected restrictions on your tablet or smartphone is necessary.

16. THE VIRTUE OF HONESTY

When Jake talks to a teenage guy about sexual struggles, he will always ask the student first how he is doing, and then once he answers, Jake will gently inquire if the student is telling the truth. No one is perfect, especially in the area of sexuality, but many of us try to hide our mistakes. Even pastors and ministry workers have weaknesses, flaws, and areas that need growth. It's best to be honest when struggles occur and deal with issues head-on rather than hiding them and fighting a losing battle.

4 THOUGHTS ON CONFLICT RESOLUTION

17.BELOW THE SURFACE

Every couple has fights that seem to repeat over and over. Compromises are made and plans of change are put in place, but behaviors somehow drift back into unhealthy territory—and before you know it, there's that same old argument again! So how does real change happen?

When facing conflict, it is so important to get below the surface of problems and really understand the deeper issues and emotions involved. Until couples identify the root cause of an issue, behaviors won't change.

The key is not to focus on the harmful behavior, but on where that behavior comes from. By tapping into these deeper places, individuals and couples can begin to heal hurts and miscommunications, satisfy unmet emotional needs, and affirm one another. When this healing takes place, very often the desired behavioral change soon follows.

18. DEMON DIALOGUES

As couples attempt connection and intimacy, they often find that it's very easy to get stuck in endless cycles of initiation and rejection, reaching out and drawing inward, trusting and feeling betrayed. Dr. Sue Johnson identifies three main types of cycles in her book *Hold Me Tight* and labels them the "Demon Dialogues." Do any of these patterns sound familiar?

1. **Find the Bad Guy**
   This cycle is about placing blame on the other person rather than resolving the issue. No one wants to admit they're wrong so both parties attack the other in order to be the "winner."

2. **The Protest Polka**
   This is both the most common and the most destructive cycle. It is a demand/withdraw type of argument where one

spouse longs for connection but tries
to get it by criticizing and attacking.
The other spouse then feels angry and
belittled, so they shut down and withdraw.
This only makes the first spouse attack
more to get a response, and around and
around it goes.

3. **Freeze and Flee**
With this cycle, when any kind of conflict
arises in the marriage, one or both of
the spouses will immediately shut down
and retreat from their partner and/or
the situation. This is also a cycle to take
seriously as it signals a real breakdown of
marital intimacy.

If you recognize any of these cycles present
in your marriage, we encourage you to find a
licensed Emotionally Focused Therapist listed
at iceeft.com. EFT is a new type of therapy
that helps couples experience freedom from
these Demon Dialogues and creates a bonded,
emotionally satisfying marriage.

19. PEANUT BUTTER...

Living in close quarters with another person brings to light many hilarious and annoying quirks. When you live with a roommate, there is always the possibility of escape. Not so with a spouse! Each couple has unique ways to work through these issues, but the way that works best for us is "Peanut Butter."

"Peanut Butter" is code for "Please pay attention to what I'm saying. It's not a joke; I'm being serious." This little phrase has come in handy over the years. It's been used to stop a streak of unwelcome tickling, let a spouse know they were being too sarcastic, and helped one of us realize that shutting cabinet doors was actually important. A phrase like "Peanut Butter" can help couples learn to pay attention when it really counts.

20. ...AND JELLY

What is one of the hardest things for spouses to do? The answer: Pause in the middle of a fight, take a deep breath, and consider the other person's perspective.

Our counselors had us say "Jelly" to help with this important habit. When we find ourselves in an argument with escalating emotions, "Jelly" serves as a verbal pause button. It means we need to physically separate and take time to calm down, identify our own feelings, and then try to see the situation from the other person's perspective. When we come back together, it is often with changed hearts and minds. Sometimes this code word works and sometimes it doesn't. "Jelly" is not meant to be a fix-all, but it's a useful tool in the arsenal of healthy conflict-resolution options for couples. What works best for you and your spouse to de-escalate arguments?

3 THINGS TO CONSIDER ABOUT DECISION-MAKING

21. STRATEGIZE

There is no right or wrong way for couples to make decisions. Every marriage will be different in how difficult choices are handled. There is, however, one key to good decision-making: being on the same page. Couples should agree on a plan for how decisions will be handled in the future. This way, when the tough decisions come, there will be a mutually agreed-upon strategy for tackling them together. This method brings couples together in the face of adversity, rather than pulling them apart in disagreement and arguments.

22. PEOPLE CHANGE

As much as we'd all like the person we married to stay exactly the same for the rest of their life, realistically this is not possible.

Everybody changes. As life hits us with new experiences, we evolve in our beliefs, habits, and opinions. Couples need to exercise grace and understanding with each other as the years of their marriage pass by. Good communication is also important. People aren't mind readers. Spouses need to communicate with each other as their thoughts and feelings about issues shift and then exercise patience while their loved one is processing this new information.

23. THE POWER OF PRAYER

Prayer is vital to healthy decision-making. In Matthew 7:7 Jesus says, *"Keep on asking, and you will receive what you ask for. Keep on seeking, and you will find. Keep on knocking, and the door will be opened to you."* In our marriage, we have found these words to be true. Every single time we've humbly and honestly asked God for guidance and then listened for his response, we've eventually found ourselves in agreement about the decision. Allowing God to lead and direct choices relieves a substantial amount of pressure and brings couples together under their always wise and all-knowing Father. Need to make a decision? Pray about it!

3 REASONS WHY PHYSICAL HEALTH IS IMPORTANT IN MARRIAGE

24. BALANCED DIETS

Eating well improves overall health and mood, and it does wonders for waistlines. Even though it might seem like food has nothing to do with marriage, a balanced, healthy diet is actually very important to marital satisfaction. Healthy eating prolongs your lifespan, gives you more energy, helps to regulate emotions, and prevents disease. All these things are good for marriage and for a healthy sex life. When spouses take care of their bodies, they are saying to each other, "I care about how I look and feel. I want to be desirable to you, and I want to be healthy for you so that I will be around for a long time."

25. WORK IT OUT

Whether at the gym, at home, or outdoors, maintaining physical fitness is great for self-confidence, well-being, and a healthy sex life. Working out at a gym can get expensive, especially when couples are living on a ministry budget. Workout DVDs or running outside are cheap alternatives to a gym membership. Jake has also been using Kinect for Xbox® along with a couple of workout video games that are customizable. Changing up workout routines is a good way to keep things fresh, active, and fun.

26. SHARE A HOBBY

Another way to stay in shape and to foster quality time in your marriage is to find some physical activities you can enjoy together. Go for a long bike ride around your neighborhood.

Find a mountain or hiking trail nearby and take along a picnic for lunch. Or buy or rent some kayaks and spend a morning out on the water. Things like this will not only help keep you and your spouse healthy, but also will lead to shared memories, new conversations, and bonding experiences.

4 KINDS OF MARRIAGE-SAVING SUPPORT EVERY COUPLE SHOULD HAVE

27. COUNSELING

Licensed marriage and family counselors are invaluable to couples during the inevitable struggles they will face. For many years a stigma has surrounded counseling; we think that only crazy people go to therapy. Thankfully, this damaging mindset is changing as many couples realize how wise it is to get help when you need it. Sometimes you and your spouse can't agree upon certain issues and you need a third party for a short while to guide you to unity. Other times unexpected challenges will present themselves, such as a loss of a job or parent, the sickness of a child, drama with extended family, or other significant events. Counseling is a tool to facilitate healthy communication, and we can honestly say that it has saved our marriage many times.

28. MENTORS

Mentors and relationships with older people really matter when it comes to keeping a marriage together. There is so much that younger couples haven't lived through yet, and they desperately need to know how other people made it through. Sometimes solutions can only come from mentors because we get stuck in endless circles of emotion and hurt and we need older, wiser couples to speak into our marriages.

No matter what age you are, be persistent in reaching out to older folks and asking them to mentor you individually and as a couple. It doesn't even have to be an official "mentoring relationship." It works just as well to have older, more experienced people over for dinner and learn through in-depth conversations about what makes their marriage work.

29. SMALL GROUPS

Small groups are important to marriages because they foster community and friendships. When problems hit, many couples feel alone. But if they are part of a tightly knit small group, they can share their struggles and usually will discover they are not the only ones facing hardships. Both spouses should feel comfortable in the group and with sharing honestly. We would also suggest finding a group (maybe at another church) where ministry couples are not expected to lead or prepare, but simply can show up and participate. This prevents burnout and gives couples a place to be ministered to instead of ministering.

30. SENIOR PASTOR

Every couple with one or both spouses in a ministry position must decide how to interact with their senior pastor. Is the pastor a boss, a colleague, or a friend? How couples answer this question will dictate what kind of a resource their senior pastor can be to them. Some senior pastors desire to let go of the boss mentality to serve and counsel other staff like they would anyone else in the church. Some shift between the roles of boss, mentor, and friend very well and will offer support as well as leadership. Others will only want to be seen as the boss, and ministry staff must seek professional counselors or elders in the church for marital support. Whatever role the senior pastor plays, couples should do their best to be respectful and understanding, while making sure they receive the support they need.

6 WAYS TO CONNECT SPIRITUALLY

31. UNDERSTAND YOUR DIFFERENCES

One thing many couples assume when they get married is that they will experience a relationship with God in exactly same way. In his book *Sacred Pathways*, author Gary Thomas explores nine specific ways in which people connect with God. Some people approach God more intellectually and read their Bible alongside a commentary. Others connect best through liturgy and traditions. Still others feel closest to God through ascetics and experiences such as nature walks or writing in a journal.

There is not one correct, formulaic way to connect with God, and it is important to be sensitive to our differences. We have learned to have open communication and flexibility in our marriage when it comes to spending time with God together. Sometimes we talk deeply about a

Bible passage or sermon, which Jake likes, and other times we go for a hike and silently reflect on God's creation, which is what Melissa prefers.

Celebrating differences allows couples to experience God in new and refreshing ways, while also drawing them closer together. Spouses will often see God from new perspectives, and their understanding of him and how he works will go to a much deeper level.

32. WORSHIP ELSEWHERE

When one spouse is a ministry employee, it can be rather difficult to worship together. Even if your church has multiple services and you can attend one together as a family, many times both spouses still have to be "on" rather than fully engaged in the worship experience. We have found it extremely helpful to our spiritual growth to involve ourselves in a few things outside of our home church:

- Attend a service at another church that meets at a different time from your own.

- Take a class offered by another church, or audit a Bible class at a Christian college or seminary.

- Regularly watch or listen to podcasts or sermons together at home.

- Listen to worship music together in the car.

33. DO DEVOTIONS TOGETHER

Devotions are important. They are times to set aside the worries and cares of the day, week, or month and focus on God together. This time will look different for each marriage. One couple we know spends a few minutes every morning reading *Our Daily Bread* together before starting the day. Others purchase couples devotionals (we highly recommend *Closer* by Jim and Cathy Burns) to read and discuss once a week. It can also be helpful to schedule a special date night to share what you both have been learning in your individual devotional times.

34. TANDEM PRAYER

Whether it's Christian-based research or a sociological study from a secular institution, the conclusion about praying together as a couple seems to be the same: The more often a couple prays together, the healthier the relationship will be. And the chances for divorce plummet. Times of prayer should be a "must" in your relationship.

Whether you pray out loud or silently, read something from the *Book of Common Prayer*, or use a prayer journal, pray before meals, or pause in the midst of a difficult situation, prayer should be an integral part of your marriage.

35. SERVE TOGETHER

Whether it is a one-day event such as helping at a soup kitchen, something bigger such as going on a week-long mission trip (as participants, not leaders), or anything in between, taking time to serve in tandem can be a great way to grow spiritually closer to each other, to God, and to the surrounding community.

36. GO AWAY

Ministry conferences can be spiritually refreshing and reconnecting for a marriage relationship. Heading to the Simply Youth Ministry Conference or another like it can be a great way to worship together and recharge. Relevant seminars, connecting with other ministry workers, and quality time together are just some of the benefits of these types of conferences.

You can also get away together for a spiritual retreat. Many monasteries and retreat centers offer programs where couples can spend focused time praying, reading Scripture, and refreshing their connection to God. Wealthy church members might also have vacation homes they'd be willing to lend out to be used by church staff for spiritual retreats.

SECTION 2

BALANCING MARRIAGE AND MINISTRY

Ministry is a 24/7 gig. There are always students to call, parents to appease, questions to answer, volunteers to train, and events to plan. These demands usually spill over from work hours into personal time and can overwhelm a marriage. It can be very hard to learn and enforce healthy boundaries. Here are the things we try to establish in our own marriage to make sure our relationship stays strong.

5 THOUGHTS ON TAMING THE MINISTRY TONGUE

37. LIMIT MINISTRY CONVERSATIONS

Ministry workers need to talk about their day just like everyone else, but because a church is made up of a large quantity of people and a never-ending supply of drama and problems, it's best to place limits on sharing. Agree on a set amount of time to decompress with your spouse once you get home, and then dispense with church topics for the remainder of the evening. A walk together is a great time to talk about ministry, and it has the added bonus of a definitive beginning and end. When the walk is done, so is the church talk.

38. DECOMPRESS

After a full day of ministry, especially one that is full of stressful situations, take a longer route home or find a nearby park to sit in for 10-15 minutes. Take this time to decompress, listen to the radio, sit and process the events of the day, talk on the phone with a friend, or spend some quiet time in prayer. Making space for decompression can greatly help ministry workers shift their focus from church back to their own self, spouse, and children waiting for their attention at home.

39. SPOUSES DON'T NEED TO KNOW EVERYTHING

This has been one of the most difficult things for us to learn. When it comes to frustrations or conflict in the church, the non-ministry (non-staffed) spouse doesn't need to know every detail and incident. Sharing every issue with them is one of the quickest ways to ruin your spouse's feelings about church, and it can have a dramatic impact on their ability to worship and be spiritually fed there.

Unless a job is in jeopardy, ministry workers should keep negative situations to themselves, at least at first. The staff spouse should try to pray about what upsetting thing happened that day, talk to other people, or spend time processing the situation on their own. Half of the time they'll realize the issue isn't that important. The other half of the time, the issue will be important to share, but the ministry worker will be able to communicate things in a way that is less emotional and non-reactive.

40. TALK TO SOMEONE ELSE

Jake has a mentor he meets with regularly, and together they share thoughts about life and ministry. His father is also a pastor, so Jake can run church-related questions and concerns by him as well. Both of these men help absorb and process some of the ministry conversations Jake needs to have so that they don't all happen at home. Talking to other people besides your spouse about ministry will create a more balanced marriage and personal life.

41. BE INTENTIONAL ABOUT OTHER TOPICS

Spend a few minutes each day intentionally investigating what is happening in the world outside of church and ministry. We have found it valuable to read news articles, listen to the radio, surf the Web, and read interesting books. It can get really boring to talk about Christianity *all* the time. Melissa likes to say, "God is in politics, literature, music, fashion, art, and sports just a much as he is in church. Don't worry, you won't hurt his feelings if you talk about one of those things instead."

7 REASONS SABBATH IS IMPORTANT

42. TAKE ONE DAY OFF AND ONE FLEX DAY A WEEK

Jesus said in Mark 2:27, *"The Sabbath was made to meet the needs of people, and not people to meet the requirements of the Sabbath."*

Every pastor and ministry worker should have one full day of Sabbath rest each week. This means no phone calls, no work emails, no meetings, and no church events. We also think it's important to try to avoid doing errands or paying bills on this day. The Sabbath day should be for couples to relax. Go hiking, stay in bed all day, or visit a museum—anything other than work stuff. It doesn't matter what day of the week couples decide their Sabbath will be; it's only important that the day happens. This rest will not only benefit spouses as individuals and their marriages, but it also will actually greatly enhance your ministry. A good pastor is a rested pastor.

On top of the Sabbath day each week, a ministry worker also should have what we call a "flex day." This flex day is also a scheduled day off from work, but answering phone calls and checking email are allowed. We also do our best to reserve the flex day for any errands, housework, bill paying, or other things that need to get done. And sometimes the flex day is swallowed up by a ministry event. The key is to have this day set aside for responsibilities so that couples can truly enjoy their Sabbath rest.

43. TRIP PROTOCOL

Trips and retreats can be fantastic times with students, but they can also be draining and exhausting. After a trip of three days or more, ministry workers should do their best to take at least one extra day off from work to rest and recover. This is important for energy levels, focus, and overall health.

44. PAID VACATION

In our opinion, a full-time youth worker should have a minimum of three weeks' paid vacation per year. For the sake of their marriages, families, and ministries, couples should take all the time off that a church offers. Seriously, it's OK. The ministry will continue to run just fine. It's important to get away, refresh, and have focused time for your marriage and family. Personally, we've found that going away twice a year is really important for our marriage. The rest of the allotted vacation is then reserved for spending time with extended family during the holidays, special occasions, or emergencies. Churches need to support healthy ministry, and rest is a key component of this. If vacation is unpaid, even after a couple of years, it's OK to go to your senior pastor or finance committee and respectfully make a case as to why at least some paid vacation is important.

45. HEALTHY HOURS

In our opinion, a full-time pastor or ministry worker shouldn't work more than an average of 50 hours a week. Jake's first senior pastor shared this helpful hint: break each day into three sections—7 a.m.-noon, noon-5 p.m., and 5-10 p.m.—and then make sure to be home with your spouse and family for at least one of those chunks of time. Overworked spouses do not give as much time and energy to their marriages. But a spouse who works healthy hours will have a rested mind and body and therefore a better marriage.

46. LIMIT YOUR MINISTRY NIGHTS PER WEEK

In his book *Creating an Intimate Marriage*, Jim Burns talks about the importance of limiting "ministry nights" each week. This means nights spent out at ministry events or church meetings. Many couples find that evenings are their only time together. If too many evenings are swallowed by work, little is left for the marriage. There is no set rule for how many nights out is appropriate; it will be different for each relationship. Our limit is no more than three ministry nights out per week. Take some time to talk and pray together about what is best for your marriage, and keep in mind that whatever you decide might change as the seasons of life ebb and flow.

47. AVOID BACK-TO-BACK WEEKENDS

Another thing we try to avoid: back-to-back weekend events. The amount of time and energy that it takes to plan and execute a weekend outing or event can be taxing, and doing this two weekends in a row can be a bit much. Altering the church calendar can be daunting, but many church and program directors will be willing to work with you to move around events as long as you approach them with flexibility and respect.

48. YOU DIDN'T MARRY YOUR SMARTPHONE

One of the biggest disruptions to quality time, rest, and good communication is the ever-expanding sphere of technology. It is crucial for spouses to purposely disconnect from phones, emails, texts, social media, and the Internet at certain times in order to connect with each other. This can be very difficult for those in ministry as the demands of students and parishioners often stream in 24/7. But taking one day off from technology will help rather than hurt your ministry. It's also wise to occasionally turn off cell phones, tablets, and laptops in the evenings. This should definitely be the case if you're heading out on a date, but it's also good if you just need a quiet night in.

On our Sabbath day together, Jake turns off his cell phone, and his voicemail states that he will return calls the next day. He also designates an on-call staff member or a volunteer to stand in for him just in case any bigger issues in the ministry come up during the day off. This helps him feel that the ministry is covered and he doesn't have to check technology all day.

6 WAYS TO SURVIVE THE HOLIDAYS

49. CHURCH AND HOLIDAYS

Often pastors are expected to work during the holiday season. This can greatly affect family traditions, trips, and plans. To tend to the needs and desires of your family, we recommend that couples have some purposeful conversations with church leadership well in advance of the holiday season. What are the church's expectations during a specific holiday? Are you allowed to take time away with your family? And does that time off count as vacation time? Couples will probably have to find creative ways to meet both job requirements and the needs of family.

50. PREPARE

It sounds silly, but couples need to prepare for the holidays—especially newly married couples who often have no idea what to expect and who think everything will go smoothly and happily. About two or three months before the holiday, sit down and discuss possible plans together. Couples should talk about how they would like to celebrate the time, what their respective families might expect, and what emotions this certain holiday evokes for each spouse. As soon as you begin this conversation, we guarantee you will discover why preparation is not silly at all! There are often a barrage of conflicting expectations and emotions. If couples are not on the same page concerning plans, it will cause tension, fights, and hurt feelings all around. So take the time to talk about things beforehand and make the holidays an enjoyable time for both spouses and extended family.

51. TEAM PLAYERS

Decisions about holiday plans should always be made together, and both spouses should stick to them like glue. It's easy to let even well-meaning family members or parishioners sway opinions, but couples should do their best to keep their

word to each other above anyone else. If
conflicts or sticky situations arise, it's best to be
united in public and then discuss things later
in private. Keeping a team player attitude will
show everyone else how much you respect your
marriage and your spouse. It also will prevent
anyone from intentionally or unintentionally
driving a wedge between you and an enjoyable
holiday experience.

52. COMPROMISE

It's pretty fair to say that nobody is going to
be completely satisfied during the holidays.
A gathered group of people, large or small,
means compromise and flexibility are essential.
Couples should work together to find healthy
ways to please each other's families and then
also bear with each other when discussing their
own personal holiday expectations. The best
way to get through any holiday season is to truly
understand that everyone will have to give a
little bit.

63. BUDGET

Spending money often goes hand in hand with holiday celebrations: extra groceries to buy, presents to purchase, gas for long car trips, decorations that need to be replaced, and a zillion extra social events to attend. All these things add up, and it can be frustrating when couples have different ideas of how much or how little they want to spend. The best way to handle spending is to create a holiday budget together. And stick to it! Both partners can discuss where they'd like to spend extra money and how much they feel is appropriate. At the end of the discussion, couples should have a budget that is agreed upon by both parties. That way, spending becomes fun and not another holiday squabble.

64. HANDLE YOUR OWN FAMILY

Cross-family communication (discussing plans with in-laws) is not the smartest idea during holiday season. We've found that the best way to avoid hurt feelings and protect the holiday plans that couples have already made together is for husbands and wives to each deal with their own family. For some reason, relatives hear and understand things better from their own kin and are much more willing to accept a change in tradition when it's explained by a family member.

2 WAYS TO HAVE A LIFE OUTSIDE THE CHURCH

55. FRIENDSHIPS

It can be very easy for a ministry couple to get stuck in what we call "the ministry bubble." This bubble typically consists of a small circle of people whom both spouses come into contact with on a regular basis. They are usually either part of your church, people who work in conjunction with your church, or ministry peers in the area. These friendships are definitely important, but it's not healthy to surround yourself solely with people who have the exact same mindset and set of beliefs that you do. Couples should seek relationships with people outside of the church to gain rich friendships with all kinds of unique and wonderful people.

56. GET INVOLVED

The most obvious, yet often overlooked, way to have a life outside of the church is to get involved in a local community. Spouses can volunteer at neighborhood organizations and get to know their fellow volunteers. They can attend their children's sports games or plays, or if children are younger, take them to library storytimes or play groups and get to know other parents there. Couples could attend local theaters, seasonal festivals, town fairs, or community college classes—and make a point to engage with lots of other people outside of their church home.

SECTION 3

FINANCES

Finances are a major tension point in most marriages and continually one of the top causes of divorce. Add in an often overworked and underpaid youth worker to the mix, and money can become a real source of friction in the relationship. This section will take a look at what it means to have healthy finances on a ministry budget.

6 FINANCIAL QUESTIONS THAT COULD MAKE OR BREAK YOUR MARRIAGE

67. HOW DOES YOUR SPOUSE THINK ABOUT MONEY?

It's common for people to think that their spouse has the exact same financial philosophy they do, but that's rarely the case. It's important to understand both spouses' views on money, and the best way to do this to discuss these kinds of questions:

- What does your spouse like/dislike about the way their parents handled money?

- How does this impact the way your spouse handles money now?

- How does your spouse deal with credit cards and debt?

- What do they think the role of a budget is?

- What do they spend their money on?

- What are their future financial goals?

The answers to these questions will change throughout the entire course of a marriage as people evolve and views shift. Couples need to have open lines of communication when it comes to finances and should work hard to understand and validate the views of their spouse.

58. WHO IS RESPONSIBLE FOR WHAT?

Important questions for every couple to answer:

- Will one person pay the bills each month, or will you each pay some?

- Who is going to balance the checkbook? How often will that be done?

- Who is going to take care of deposits?

- Will grocery shopping be done together, or will one person do it?

- Who is going to set and track a budget?

Each couple needs to figure out what works best for them when it comes to financial roles. It may take time to determine this in the early days of a new marriage. Jake is better at math, so he balances the checkbook, tracks the budget, and pays bills. Melissa has a sixth sense when it comes to grocery shopping and can stay on budget with scary accuracy, so she handles those things solo. What works best for you and your spouse?

69. WHAT ABOUT BANK ACCOUNTS?

Most people expect to combine their checking and savings accounts when they get married, but bank accounts don't have to look one specific way. Some couples find it easier to manage money by having totally separate accounts and splitting the bill paying. Some have separate spending accounts but share their savings and one main joint checking.

The key here is honesty and trust. Whatever way you and your spouse decide to arrange things, make sure to talk it all over first and come up with a plan you both fully agree upon.

60. WHAT SHOULD A MONTHLY BUDGET LOOK LIKE?

Hashing out a monthly budget can really remove a lot of stress from a marriage. Setting one up isn't rocket science, which is good for those of us who are mathematically challenged.

Step #1: Determine your total monthly total income. For most people this means adding up regular paychecks. It does get trickier when one spouse has work that fluctuates. The best way to handle this is to base your monthly income off the least amount both of you make on a regular basis. It's better to budget with what you know you'll have, rather than the paycheck you hope comes in.

Step #2: Figure out your non-negotiable monthly expenses. These could include things such as rent, groceries, utilities, school loans, gas, insurance, and anything else that you both decide you just can't live without. (See Thoughts 71-73 for questions and ideas about tithing and giving.) Subtract this amount from your monthly total in Step #1.

If Step # 2's total expenses exceed the monthly income amount, it's time to start cutting. The best way to avoid financial stress and debt is to not spend more than you make!

Step #3: Once all the non-negotiable bills are accounted for, there are a number of conversations to have concerning leftover (or disposable) income:

- Are we going to give any of this money away? (Again, see Thoughts 71-73.)

- How much will we put into savings? Experts generally recommend 10 percent of each paycheck. However, deciding what to put in savings will be dictated by future goals such as buying a house, continued education costs, or having kids.

- How much will we spend on entertainment each month? This includes date nights, outings with friends, a bottle of wine after a stressful week, or whatever will help you relax and de-stress.

- Will we have personal spending allowances? How much will that be?

Step # 4: Stick to the budget! This might seem like common sense, yet so many people make budgets but never stick to them—and then wonder why debt comes knocking on their door.

If jobs or incomes change, make sure to re-address the budget. Life gets messy and budgets will often need to be tweaked to account for financial fluctuations. Also, if you miss your budget one month, try again the next! Don't throw the budget out the window just because you both failed a time or two. Healthy financial practices take time to learn; be gracious with one another and keep working at it.

61. DO WE REALLY NEED THAT?

Our Western culture often confuses "needs" with "wants." We think we need something, but we can actually survive just fine without it. As couples hash out budgets, it's crucial to understand what is a need and what is a want. This might be different for each spouse. It takes a lot of listening, compromise, and grace to make a dual budget, so couples need to approach these conversations with some deep breaths and good attitudes.

Mark Powley's book *Consumer Detox* details many instances where his family needed or wanted something, but instead of running out and buying it, they waited and asked God to provide. And God did, almost every time. It's easy to forget that God promises to give us what we need and that we can trust him to do just that. Sometimes he gives us the things we want as well!

Another great book about needs vs. wants is *Simplify* by Paul Borthwick (a former youth pastor himself). The book offers 106 ideas to help couples and families live more simply. Not all of the suggestions in the book directly impact finances—some address issues such as balancing a schedule and healthy eating habits—but many of them do talk about money. Borthwick's strategy is that when life is simpler, it costs less to sustain it.

62. WHAT ABOUT EXTRA INCOME?

Sometimes couples in ministry can find themselves in situations where finances are tight and extra income becomes necessary. To figure out if side jobs are wise for your marriage, family, and finances, consider these questions:

- Is the additional job for a season or more long term? If you're thinking long term, it may be better to first approach a current employer about a raise or look for a new job with a higher salary.

- How do you both feel about adding something extra to your schedule? Take the time to really discuss how this will impact your marriage and life together.

- Are there any ways to cut expenses so a side job isn't necessary?

Ministry is very demanding of both personal and family time. Adding side jobs to this mix can sometimes be disastrous. We advise that you try to avoid it if at all possible. But if extra income is the only solution, make sure that the side job is healthy and that you still have weekly times of rest and relaxation.

2 THOUGHTS ABOUT WHERE TO LIVE

63. FAMILY FIRST

Often pastors decide where to live based on the location of their church. However, the needs of the spouse and/or family should always come before the needs of the church. A pastor can't be "on" all the time, and spouses and families need to have their own space. Some couples will decide that living in a parsonage works well for them; others will find that they need to live a town or two over from the church. The key is to decide what kind of living situation will foster healthy boundaries and meet your personal needs *before* the ministry's needs.

64. AFFORDABILITY

If a church requires or strongly suggests that employees live in the same town or city as the church, the congregation should pay them enough to reasonably afford the cost of living there. Being part of the local community is important, but couples shouldn't bankrupt themselves to do so. It is understandable if churches can't afford higher salaries, but staff should then be free to live in a different city or town that is more affordable and commute to work.

6 WAYS TO THINK THROUGH WHAT YOU'RE WORTH

65. COMPARE YOURSELF NATIONALLY...

National church compensation books or surveys can be a great resource to help pastors, youth pastors, and church staff understand what salary they should be making. Christianity Today publishes a very thorough *Compensation Handbook for Church Staff* that provides statistical breakdowns of different types of church positions and also accounts for church size and geography. Specific to youth ministry, Group Magazine does a regular survey that pastors can use to compare their position, salary, and benefits to other youth workers around the country.

66. ...AND LOCALLY

The one downside to national surveys and statistics is that sometimes the areas surveyed can be too broad. It's difficult to provide a clear picture of the living costs for a specific place. For example, we live in the Northeast, but living costs vary widely from county to county. A ministry position in rural Maine looks very different salary-wise from a position in Fairfield County, Connecticut.

When couples are considering a job, it's a good idea to call other churches in the area and find out what their youth workers are paid. Make sure to understand job responsibilities, salary, and benefits, as well as the church and youth ministry size. We also recommend couples try to talk to the youth workers themselves and find out how they feel about their compensation packages.

67. BEWARE OF THE LEMMING EFFECT

The "Lemming Effect" is this: If churches in a particular area are all underpaying or burning out youth workers, there will be a high turnover rate and everyone will think this is normal. Churches tend to follow the patterns of other churches. So look for areas where youth workers stay long term. Employees who stay for longer periods of time show that churches are providing fair compensation packages and have healthy expectations. These are the kinds of churches and positions that you want to compare your position to.

68. TEACHERS

One of the best ways to figure out what you're worth is to find out what public school teachers make in the town where you'll work. Youth workers should make just about the same as a public school teacher. The government bases their salaries on experience, schooling, and cost of living in their particular area. You can use an online search engine to research "pay scale for [enter town or district here] teachers," or call the school district's office and get information there. The numbers are generally easy to access.

Keep in mind that a teacher's salary is based on a 10-month work calendar with about a month of vacation time. To find a comparable salary for the full year, simply divide the teacher rate by 10 months and then multiply by 12.

69. CONTRACTS

Many churches do not provide contracts for their staff, but contracts are crucial for maintaining a healthy work environment. A good contract will include things such as salary and benefits, as well as how salary increases are made, job requirements, weekly hours, and any continuing education requirements. It should also clearly communicate why one would be fired, laid off, or asked to resign. Paperwork is never fun and contract conversations can be uncomfortable to initiate, but having a contract in place will prevent a lot of heartache and confusion down the road. If you don't have a contract, we recommend talking with your senior pastor or another leader in the church about drafting one together.

70. HEALTH CARE

Health care is a touchy subject with churches. But as out-of-pocket costs soar, many ministry workers cannot afford to pay for their own health insurance. Any full-time ministry position should come with benefits; it's a matter of healthy ministry and being valued by an employer. If the church doesn't provide coverage and couples can't get insurance through a spouse's employer, here are a handful of options to discuss with your church so your family's health needs are taken care of:

- Purchase a self-employed policy—We had a season in our marriage where we did this and the church reimbursed us. It was actually cheaper than if the church took out the policy.

- Check out a health savings account—This is a tax-free savings account designated toward medical expenses. Funds can only be used for medical costs, but the balance carries over from year to year.

- Look for a consumer health cooperative in your area—These allow small businesses and not-for-profits to buy insurance together, thus lowering premiums.

3 THINGS TO CONSIDER ABOUT GIVING

71. TWO SIDES OF THE COIN

For many couples, giving is an area of tension, especially in the midst of a struggling economy.

What can make this conversation even more difficult is that there are varied interpretations of what biblical giving should look like. The most common view is that of the tithe: giving 10 percent of yearly or monthly income to the church. But even this widely accepted practice raises many questions:

- Does the 10 percent apply to income before or after taxes?

- Do you have to give the 10 percent to a local church or can you give it to a mission agency or nonprofit organization?

- If you're struggling financially, can you give less than 10 percent?

- Are extremely wealthy people obligated to give more than 10 percent?

- What if spouses disagree about tithing? Does this condemn your finances?

- What about gifts, bonuses, or other unexpected checks? Should you tithe on those as well?

It's important for couples to understand each other's ideas about giving, rather than force their own opinion. They can also talk to their parents, trusted friends, or pastors, and pray about what giving should look like for their marriage. God commands families to give, but this must be done in a united and peaceful way. Giving 10 percent is a fantastic benchmark to aim for, but don't get legalistic about it. The idea is to be generous and faithful, whatever that may look like.

72. THE RIGHT ATTITUDE

Humility is important when couples give. Marriages are edified when spouses can give joyfully, humbly, and prayerfully. Donations to church or charity should not be shouted from the rooftops. Keep each other accountable about this; it can be tempting to boast when you're being generous.

Also remember that God doesn't want 10 percent of our finances; he wants 100 percent. The money we're blessed with is a gift from God, along with the skills and talents God gave us to earn that money. As couples discuss giving, they should consider how to be good stewards of *everything* God has blessed them with, including houses, cars, clothes, food, *and* finances.

73. TAKE THE CHALLENGE

Regularly challenge each other about giving. Being a follower of Christ means radical living and stretching those comfort zones. We try to evaluate what we give every 6 to 12 months, because finances tend to shift and change. We also challenge ourselves whenever there are any extra jobs, gifts, or bonuses.

SECTION 4

THE CHURCH VS. YOUR FAMILY

We've had many moments in our marriage when we felt like our church and our family were at total odds. One senior pastor lectured Jake about our decision not to attend the annual "Family Wreath-Making Event," even though we didn't have kids, didn't have the money to pay for the wreath-making materials, and had been out doing ministry four nights already that week. Another time, an interview committee told us that it was completely unrealistic for Melissa to want to stay home when we had kids—that she'd have to work to support Jake's job as a pastor because he would be underpaid. (We arrived at Jake's current job six months later, and the church has been nothing but wonderful and supportive of Melissa.)

The truth is, churches and families don't have to be at war with one another. With preparation, wisdom, and patience, it is possible to find a church that complements and supports your family's needs.

4 WAYS TO DEAL WITH CHURCH EXPECTATIONS

74. BEWARE THE "2 FOR 1"

Sometimes churches hire one spouse and expect the other to partner in the ministry for free. Many couples thrive in these types of positions, but others don't. The call to ministry is an important one, and a spouse should not be forced into a volunteer position with expectations they may not be gifted to fulfill. Forcing a "2-for-1" position can lead to marital discord and ministry burnout, a no-win situation for everyone involved. When looking for a new position, couples should make sure to ask about expectations of the non-paid spouse.

75. PART OF IT ALL

Most churches have expectations on how a non-paid spouse will be involved with the ministry. The easiest way to understand these expectations is to bluntly ask your supervisor, head pastor, elders, or board about them. Then you can have a conversation about how the expectations may or may not fit the unique personhood and gifting of your spouse. The idea is to be respectful but firm on things that your spouse does not feel comfortable with. Spouses need to feel excited about church and get involved based on their special and unique talents.

76. SEASONAL MINISTRY

Spousal involvement will often ebb and flow as years pass and life brings new seasons and changes. Churches and ministries should be made aware of this fact so that if a spouse needs to alter their commitments for a time, it is both understood and supported.

77. PRESSURE ON THE KIDS

If couples have children, they should be aware that their kids will be affected by the ministry in some manner. The rebellious "pastor's kid" stereotype exists for a reason! However, parents can do their best to make growing up in a ministry family a good experience by putting the family's needs first. The church hired the parent, not the 8-year-old. Spend time discussing what it means to have a pastor as a parent and how this may impact school, home, friendships, and involvement at church. Ask your kids what you can do to help them navigate any pressure-filled areas or things they are struggling with. Keeping an open dialogue will let your children know that you are aware of any difficulties they might face, that you care, and that you're there for them.

4 THOUGHTS ABOUT LEADING BY EXAMPLE: FAMILY AS MINISTRY

78. MODELING MARRIAGE FOR STUDENTS

A month after we were married, Jake had the chance to attend a "Youth Ministry and Marriage" workshop with Jim Burns. One of the most important things he learned there was that the vast majority of students see their fair share of broken marriages and dysfunctional family dynamics. Burns taught that youth workers must show by example that marriages can be loving and that family can come first. Students should be aware that you're having dinner with family a certain number of nights a week, that you go on dates with your spouse, and that you spend special time with your kids. This helps students learn what healthy relationships look like and, we hope, carry that knowledge with them when they get married and have their own families.

79. APPROPRIATE PDA

Another way for couples to be examples of healthy marriage is to show appropriate PDA and loving affection for each other. Sadly, it's something many kids don't see at home. An arm behind the back or on the knee during a church service, a kiss or hug when saying goodbye, or holding hands at an event shows students that good marriages are possible. We have had many youth groupers comment on our little cheek kisses and quick hugs, but they do so with a smile and a "that's so cute!"

80. BREAKING BREAD

Invite a student, couple, or small group from the church over for a meal. Better yet, invite them over early and prepare the meal together. Breaking bread is a wonderful way for couples to be personal with those in their church. Making and eating a meal together is one of the oldest community-building practices in existence. This lets parishioners get to know you as real people and also see what a healthy marriage and family life look like.

81. BEATING THE MINISTRY PERSONA

Pastors are called to a higher standard in both their professional and personal lives because they have the responsibility of leading others. But this doesn't mean that you should be fake. It's easy to perpetuate the "ministry persona" by pretending that nothing bad happens, life is easy, sin is nonexistent, and church is wonderful. This isn't real. Pastors sin. They're human. They struggle with doubts, sometimes swear, may drink beer, have sex with their spouse, and enjoy many other things besides church. (Gasp!) Being yourself and loving who God uniquely made you to be is the most authentic way to do ministry. It also takes the pressure off you and your spouse to portray a certain type of image, one that may not line up with who you are as a couple.

4 MUSTS FOR FINDING A JOB THAT FITS YOUR FAMILY

82. A SPOUSE'S CALLING

When it comes to vocation, ministry is usually considered a "higher calling." But the vocation of a non-ministry spouse is just as important to God and vital to the church as a whole. There are many parts to the body, and we all should work together, using the unique talents and positions God has placed us in to glorify him and spread the message of Jesus Christ.

Before a spouse interviews for a church position, couples should take time to pray and talk about individual calling and giftedness. Prayerfully consider how both your vocations might mesh or possibly conflict. Commitment means working together to support each other and requires "give" by both parties.

When you do interview for a ministry position, it's crucial to communicate your spouse's calling and how that dictates your specific family expectations. Finding a church where your spouse can pursue their desired vocation as you pursue yours will create a healthy and mutually supportive marriage.

83. YOUR FAMILY'S FINANCIAL GOALS

Financial planning is fundamental in a ministry marriage, as Section 3 of this book addressed. Before applying for any job, it's important to discuss your family's financial expectations, based on your unique career goals. Money is not the reason anyone gets into ministry (nor should it be). The focus is on serving God, but wisdom, a little forethought, and a bit of backbone will be invaluable as you and your spouse consider the financial implications of accepting or rejecting paid ministry positions.

84. FAMILY VALUES

We discussed common expectations that churches have for families in Thoughts 74-77, but what are your family's expectations of the church? Before looking for a job, spouses and children should talk together about what kind of church you all want, how you'd like to be involved, and what kinds of support you'd like to receive. There is no perfect job or church, but there are many different kinds of positions, so it's wise to decide what key things your family would like to see.

85. A HEALTHY LIFESTYLE

In his book *Simple Solutions for Families in the Fast Lane*, author (and former youth pastor) Tim Smith explains that every person has a natural pace of life—what he calls a "Heart Print." Some people like life to be fast-paced and ever-changing, while others like it slow and predictable. Every person and every couple has different rhythms of rest, work, and play that suit their individual needs. Before interviewing for a position, couples should decide what a healthy lifestyle means for their marriage and then seek a position that will support those views.

SECTION 5

THE DARKER SIDE OF THE CHURCH

These are the things that not many want to discuss but that every seasoned ministry worker either knows about or has experienced firsthand. Churches are made up of people, and even wonderful Christian people sin. There are just as many problems, frustrations, hurt feelings, blowouts, failures, and nasty little secrets in ministry jobs as there are in secular ones. So how do you deal with them?

3 UNEXPECTED EXPECTATIONS

86. EXPECT CHURCH POLITICS

As young, idealistic youth workers, we dive into ministry excited to work with other Christians and change the world for Christ. Many of us are shocked to find people who are more than capable of lying, manipulating, gossiping, pulling power plays, and controlling others. Unfortunately, this is a dynamic in many churches. Playing the politics game can really stress out a marriage. Often spouses are called upon to play a role in these issues, whether they're told to fulfill leadership expectations or forced to agree with policies or programs they don't really support. You will encounter controlling people in churches, just like everywhere else in the world. Couples need to decide when it's wise to keep quiet and when it's time to stand up against politics. We can't lie: This is an ever-changing, ever-involving issue that requires spouses to work as a team. Support each other in the face of church politics, and above all, keep your focus on God.

87. EXPECT TO FAIL

At the Willow Creek Leadership Summit in 2012, Jake heard author Patrick Lencioni tell a story about Southwest Airlines. The company responded to a customer's scathing criticisms with a simple email saying, "We'll miss you."

Churches and ministry leaders everywhere need to send more "We'll miss you" emails. There's no way to please every single person in your church or ministry. It's impossible. You will always fail. Both the ministry worker and their spouse should do their best to fulfill expectations in healthy ways. But after that, let criticism roll off your back. Don't bring other people's discontent into your marriage or hearts. There will always be unhappy people in churches, and what matters more is that both your personhood and marriage are strong.

88. EXPECT TO FIND OUT SOMETHING NEGATIVE ABOUT LEADERSHIP

Aren't there things in your own past or present that are dark? Faults you don't want anyone to know about, sin battles that you struggle with? You're a real person, and so are all the other ministry workers around you. It can be disheartening to learn something negative about a co-worker, lead pastor, or board member, but try to extend the grace and forgiveness you'd want if someone found out about one of your sins. Couples will have to be prayerful about what kinds of things should be forgotten and what constitutes sin that is too detrimental or serious to ignore. This would include any kind of illegal transgressions, adultery, or things that would harm individuals or the church. If issues like this come to your attention, tell a trusted member of the church leadership and/or the authorities, if the situation warrants. Be prayerful and wise about any action that you take. And for those instances that aren't so serious, the best course of action is to forgive and forget.

2 THOUGHTS ON OPPOSITE-GENDER CO-WORKERS/ STUDENTS/PARISHIONERS

89. SET BOUNDARIES

Setting boundaries when meeting with students, parents, or volunteers of the opposite gender is a must. Here are a handful of boundaries we have found helpful:

- Whenever possible, have adult men meet with guys and adult women meet with girls.

- Avoid driving alone with a member of the opposite gender at all costs.

- If you have to meet with someone of the opposite gender, whether a student or a volunteer, meet him or her at a local coffee shop or other public place.

- If you need to meet at the church due to a sensitive topic, meet in a room or office that has large windows so that anyone walking by can see you at all times.

- Avoid emails and texts that could become too personal. Give your spouse your email and social media passwords so they have access to all electronic messages.

90. OVERCOMMUNICATE

Youth workers will have times in their ministry when they cannot avoid being alone with a member of the opposite gender. The best way to deal with these situations is to overcommunicate with your spouse and other workers.

Call your spouse, another volunteer, or even your senior pastor when you know there will be one of these times. Let them know where you and the student, parishioner, or volunteer will be and how long you'll be there. Check in again with the same person after the meeting or ride has ended.

Always take time to listen to your spouse about any opposite-gender co-workers, committee members, parishioners, volunteers, or students that they might feel uncomfortable about you being alone with. Spouses should be allowed to voice any concerns. Limiting time with a certain person is more than worth it for the sake of your marriage.

THE CARDINAL RULE ON FRIENDSHIPS IN THE CHURCH

91. KEEP CHURCH POLITICS OUT

Avoid discussing the latest gossip, leadership issues, budget talks, or pastoral gaffs with church friends—you risk hurting someone, losing the friendship, or disrespecting your superiors in a major way. There will always be issues, drama, politics, and problems swirling about in the daily life of a church, and everybody loves to talk about those things. But pastors and ministry couples should stay out of these conversations when they occur. There are countless other topics to discuss and other ways to connect deeply with your church friends. Work on building and maintaining these friendships without focusing on your shared church home.

4 THOUGHTS ON WHEN TO LEAVE AND WHEN TO STAY

92. LISTEN TO YOUR SPOUSE

Pastors and youth workers often fail to realize they're heading toward burnout. Burnout creeps up on ministry workers, who have everyone else's needs at the forefront of their minds instead of their own.

If your spouse voices concerns about unhealthy behavior or things they see leading to burnout, seriously consider what they say. Your spouse knows you like no other and has your best interests at heart. If concerns are voiced, ask your spouse what could be changed to help you avoid burnout and return to healthy living. If your spouse thinks that it might be time for a change in job or position, realize that they're saying this out of love, and do not immediately dismiss the idea. God has placed your spouse in your life for a reason, and often that reason is to help you discern problem areas and facilitate change.

93. INNER CIRCLE

Have a group of trusted friends and advisers who can counsel you as a couple when difficult decisions present themselves. This group should be unbiased and have no personal or emotional ties to your church. They should be looking out for your best interests and must be able to be honest about both the pros and cons of staying or leaving. Calling is important in ministry, but sometimes to discern a calling you need to listen to the voices around you. God can use trusted friends and family to help guide you down the right path.

94. THE GRASS ISN'T ALWAYS GREENER

Melissa once blogged: "The grass is always greener from far away because distance makes things go fuzzy. It's not until you're standing on the lawn that you look down and see the bare spots, ants, and piles of dog poop." It's tempting to think that there will be fewer problems at the next church or ministry position. Sometimes it will even seem that way for a while, but every church has its own set of issues and difficult people. Even when it's the right time to walk away from a position, expect to encounter new challenges wherever you go. Allow God to lead you from place to place rather than running away from demanding circumstances.

95. IT'S OK TO LEAVE BECAUSE OF MONEY

It's amazing how many churches, pastors, and lay people expect that ministry workers will be financially strapped. It's almost like everyone thinks that suffering for the Lord in this way is actually part of what it means to be a pastor or youth worker. While no one gets into the ministry for the money, individuals and families should be paid a fair wage for their labors.

If your church cannot provide a fair or reasonable salary, it is OK to leave because of this. It is OK to leave because you're having a baby and your wife or husband wants to stay at home. It is OK to leave if financial strain is beginning to affect your marriage. But before you do, pray and consider what God is calling you to do, how you're currently handling your finances, if there are ways you can change, and what kind of a position/salary would be the healthiest for your unique needs. Many times God calls us to sacrifice our money, but that does not mean God always expects pastors to be underpaid and stressed out.

4 THINGS TO HELP YOU SURVIVE BURNOUT OR BEING FIRED

96. AVOID "IF ONLY'S"

If you and your spouse have left a church or position before, try to avoid the "if only's." The "if only's" are when people ruminate on things that have been gone badly. Dwelling on past faults will only lead to bitterness. Try to avoid rehashing past negative situations with your spouse. If there have been hurt feelings, give those feelings to God, work on forgiveness, learn from any mistakes that have been made, and move forward with whatever kind of position you are in now. Letting go is difficult, especially if you feel that you've been wronged, but ruminating will only hinder your ministry, not prosper it.

97. HOW IT LOOKS

Bob Whittet, one of Jake's professors at Gordon College, told youth ministry students that when it comes to leadership, "Worry about your own integrity and let God worry about your reputation." As hard as it may be, if you burn out or are fired from a position, we would challenge you to take this advice to heart. These situations can get very messy, but you are not responsible for what the church does or says; you are only responsible for how you react and respond. Prayerfully seek God's wisdom and direction, and keep your mouth shut when you want to say retaliatory or gossipy things. This silence might hurt your reputation, but God will honor your integrity and restore you—or give you an even better reputation down the road.

98. NOT THE SAME

When you have been hurt by a church or its leadership, it can be easy to believe that church as a whole is messed up. (See Dan Kimball's *They Like Jesus but Not the Church*.) Yes, churches are made up of sinners and things will always be less than perfect, but many churches are doing the best they can to be healthy. Couples who struggle with hurt, anger, and disillusionment as a result of burnout or being fired should seek professional counseling. A great Christian counselor will help both spouses to work through emotions, heal wounds, and provide hope that it is possible to find healthy church communities.

99. MARRIAGE BANDAGES

When burnout hits or you find yourself unexpectedly fired from a ministry position, it's easy to let your marriage fall by the wayside in favor of more pressing demands such as personal health and finding a new job. When you're at the lowest point, things become self-centered really fast. It can be tempting to use surface-level "bandages" to fix the often deep and devastating marital issues that firing or burnout produces. Avoid the mentality that everything is fine in your marriage. Don't shy away from conflict by buying gifts, planning getaway trips, disappearing into technology, or plunging yourself into busyness. Instead, seek out a licensed marriage counselor, face your problems by talking about them as a couple, work on your communication, share your struggles with trusted friends and family, and go back to the basics. Concentrate on healthy practices and connections with each other.

APPENDIX

OUR TOP 15 MARRIAGE BOOKS FOR FURTHER READING

1. *Hold Me Tight: Seven Conversations for a Lifetime of Love* by Dr. Sue Johnson

2. *Creating an Intimate Marriage: Rekindle Romance Through Affection, Warmth and Encouragement* by Jim Burns

3. *The Seven Principles for Making Marriage Work: A Practical Guide From the Country's Foremost Relationship Expert* by John Gottman

4. *Married to Distraction: Restoring Intimacy and Strengthening Your Marriage in an Age of Interruption* by Edward M. Hallowell, M.D., and Sue Hallowell, LICSW

5. *His Needs, Her Needs: Building an Affair-Proof Marriage* by Willard E. Harley Jr.

6. *The Five Love Languages: The Secret to Love That Lasts* by Gary Chapman

7. *Closer: Devotions to Draw Couples Together* by Jim and Cathy Burns

8. *Love & Respect: The Love She Most Desires; The Respect He Desperately Needs* by Emerson Eggerichs

9. *Fit to be Tied: Making Marriage Last a Lifetime* by Bill and Lynne Hybels

10. *Have a New Husband by Friday: How to Change His Attitude, Behavior and Communication in 5 Days* by Dr. Kevin Leman

11. *Hooked: New Science on How Casual Sex is Affecting Our Children* by Joe S. McIlhaney Jr., M.D., and Freda McKissic Bush, M.D. (This isn't a book about marriage, but if you translate their research to marriage, it has profound implications about the importance of sex in relationships.)

12. *Every Man's Battle: Winning the War on Sexual Temptation One Victory at a Time* by Stephen Arterburn and Fred Stoeker